Poor Richard's Almanack

Poor Richard's Almanack

Benjamin Franklin's Best Sayings

With Numerous Old
Wood Engravings by
Anonymous Contemporaries
of Poor Richard

Edited by Dean Walley

HALLMARK EDITIONS

Poor Richard's Almanack

Mankind are very odd Creatures: One Half censure what they practice, the other half practice what they censure; the rest always say and do as they ought.

Think of three Things – whence you came, where you are going, and to Whom you must account.

Make haste slowly.

Enjoy the present hour, be mindful of the past; And neither fear nor wish the approaches of the last.

He that falls in love with himself, will have no rivals.

Fear to do ill, and you need fear nought else.

Tomorrow I'll reform,
                    the fool does say;
Today itself's too late;
                    – the wise did yesterday.

Little Strokes, fell great Oaks.

To be humble to superiors is duty, to equals courtesy, to inferiors nobleness.

None are deceived, but they that confide.

Content makes poor men rich; Discontent makes rich men poor.

Fish and Visitors stink after three days.

There are no ugly loves, nor handsome prisons.

If you would have guests merry with cheer, be so yourself, or so at least appear.

The worst wheel of the cart makes the most noise.

Necessity never made a good bargain.

Be slow in choosing a friend, slower in changing.

Let all Men know thee, but no man know thee thoroughly: Men freely ford that see the shallows.

None but the well-bred man knows how to confess a fault, or acknowledge himself in an error.

Hear no ill of a friend, nor speak any of an enemy.

Three may keep a secret, if two of them are dead.

When there's no Law, there's no Bread.

Beware of the young doctor and the old barber.

Take counsel in wine, but resolve afterwards in water.

'Tis easy to see, hard to foresee.

Nor eye in a letter, nor hand in a purse, nor ear in the secret of another.

Those who in quarrels interpose, must often wipe a bloody nose.

Hear Reason, or she'll make you feel her.

The most exquisite Folly is made of Wisdom spun too fine.

An empty bag cannot stand upright.

Tricks and treachery are the practice of fools that have not wit enough to be honest.

Fear not death; for the sooner we die, the longer shall we be immortal.

Observe all men; thyself most.

Who is rich? He that rejoices in his Portion.

Well done is better than well said.

Speak with contempt of none,
              from slave to king,
The meanest Bee hath,
              and will use, a sting.

Industry pays Debts, Despair increases them.

At 20 years of age the will reigns; at 30 the wit; at 40 the judgment.

If you would keep your secret from an enemy, tell it not to a friend.

Genius without Education is like Silver in the Mine.

There are three Things extremely hard: Steel, a Diamond, and to know one's self.

Pride is as loud a Beggar as Want, and a great deal more saucy.

If evils come not, then our fears are vain;
And if they do, fear but augments the pain.

Great beauty, great strength, and great riches are really and truly of no great use; a right heart exceeds all.

Man's tongue is soft, and bone doth lack; Yet a stroke therewith may break a man's back.

To bear other people's afflictions, every one has courage and enough to spare.

A true Friend is the best Possession.

A lie stands on one leg, truth on two.

The Things which hurt, instruct.

Search others for their virtues, thyself for thy vices.

Anger is never without a Reason, but seldom with a good One.

He that would have a short Lent, let him borrow money to be repaid at Easter.

He that waits upon fortune, is never sure of a dinner.

Tongue double, brings Trouble.

People who are wrapped up in themselves make small packages.

A little House well fill'd, a little Field well till'd, and a little Wife well will'd, are great riches.

We are not so sensible of the greatest Health as of the least Sickness.

Men and melons are hard to know.

Beware of meat twice boil'd, and an old foe reconcil'd.

The heart of the fool is in his mouth, but the mouth of the wise man is in his heart.

Love your Neighbor; yet don't pull down your Hedge.

Approve not of him who commends all you say.

The Bell calls others to Church, but it-self never minds the Sermon.

You may delay, but Time will not.

Blame-all and Praise-all are two block-heads.

Take this remark from Richard,
               poor and lame,
Whate'er's begun in Anger,
                  ends in Shame.

Where there's marriage without love, there will be love without marriage.

When Reason preaches, if you don't hear her she'll box your Ears.

If man could have Half his Wishes, he would double his Troubles.

Children and Princes will quarrel for Trifles.

Haste makes Waste.

For Age and Want save while you may; No morning Sun lasts a whole Day.

He that hath no Ill-Fortune will be troubled with Good.

Many Princes sin with David, but few repent with him.

A Child thinks 20 Shillings and 20 Years can scarce ever be spent.

Early to bed and early to rise, makes a man healthy, wealthy, and wise.

Diligence is the mother of good luck.

Virtue & Happiness are Mother & Daughter.

Nothing brings more pain than too much pleasure; nothing more bondage than too much liberty.

If you would not be forgotten, as soon as you are dead and rotten, either write things worth reading, or do things worth the writing.

Forewarn'd, forearm'd.

Since thou art not sure of a Minute, throw not away an Hour.

As we must account for every idle Word, so we must for every idle Silence.

God helps them that help themselves.

'Tis easier to suppress the first Desire, than to satisfy all that follow it.

The Proud hate Pride – in others.

If you'd have a servant that you like, serve yourself.

Is there anything men take more pains about than to make themselves un-happy?

Nothing is so popular as goodness.

The rotten apple spoils his companion.

Let thy Discontents be Secrets.

Great Estates may venture more; Little Boats must keep near Shore.

'Tis great Confidence in a Friend to tell him your Faults, greater to tell him his.

In escaping from Fire, a Woman, or an Enemy, the wise man will walk, not run.

The Wolf sheds his Coat once a Year, his Disposition never.

The honest Man takes Pains, and then enjoys Pleasures; the knave takes Pleasure, and then suffers Pains.

When a Friend deals with a Friend, Let the bargain be clear and well penn'd, That they may continue Friends to the End.

Danger is a Sauce for Prayers.

Ill Customs & bad Advice are seldom forgotten.

Let thy child's first lesson be obedi-
ence, and the second will be what thou
wilt.

When you taste Honey, remember
Gall.

Content is the Philosopher's Stone, that
turns all it touches into Gold.

When you're an Anvil, hold you still;
when you're a Hammer, strike your
fill.

A true great Man will neither trample
on a worm nor sneak to an Emperor.

Love your Enemies, for they tell you
your faults.

A long Life may not be good enough, but a good Life is long enough.

He is a Governor that governs his Passions, and he is a Servant that serves them.

Virtue may not always make a Face handsome, but Vice will certain make it ugly.

Rob not God, nor the Poor, lest thou ruin thyself; the Eagle snatcht a Coal from the Altar, but it fired her Nest.

A false Friend and a Shadow attend only while the Sun shines.

The end of Passion is the beginning of Repentance.

Be civil to all; sociable to many; familiar with few; Friend to one; Enemy to none.

Pardoning the Bad, is injuring the Good.

Tomorrow every Fault is to be amended; but that Tomorrow never comes.

Vice knows she's ugly, so puts on her Mask.

Pride breakfasted with Plenty, dined with Poverty, supped with Infamy.

Proportion your Charity to the strength of your Estate, or God will Proportion your Estate to the Weakness of your Charity.

The Royal Crown cures not the Head-
ache.

The doors of Wisdom are never shut.

How few there are who have courage
enough to own their Faults, or resolu-
tion enough to mend them!

Who has deceiv'd thee so oft as thy self?

He that can compose himself, is wiser
than he that composes books.

Fine linen, girls, and gold so bright,
Choose not to take by candle light.

The use of money is all the advantage there is in having money.

He that goes far to marry, will either deceive or be deceived.

There's many witty men whose brains can't fill their bellies.

Ah simple Man! when a boy two precious jewels were given thee, Time and good Advice; one thou hast lost, and the other thrown away.

Experience keeps a dear school, yet Fools will learn in no other.

Have you somewhat to do to-morrow, do it today.

Speak and speed: the close mouth catches no flies.

An open foe may prove a curse; but a pretended friend is worse.

Let thy maid-servant be faithful, strong, and homely.

Wealth is not his that has it, but his that enjoys it.

In a discreet man's mouth a public thing is private.

Wish not so much to live long, as to live well.

If you have time, don't wait for time.

There's none deceived but he that trusts.

Eat to please thyself, but dress to please others.

There is much difference between imitating a good man, and counterfeiting him.

Wink at small faults – remember thou hast great ones.

Great Good-nature, without Prudence,
is a great Misfortune.

Do me the favor to deny me at once.

He that would live in peace and at ease,
must not speak all he knows,
nor judge all he sees.

The poor man must walk to get meat
for his stomach, the rich man to get
a stomach for his meat.

Great talkers should be cropp'd, for
they have no need of ears.

He that hath a Trade, hath an Estate.

Each year one vicious habit rooted out, in time might make the worst man good throughout.

Hunger is the best Pickle.

'Tis hard (but glorious) to be poor and honest.

An empty Sack can hardly stand upright; but if it does, 'tis a stout one!

He that spills the Rum loses that only; He that drinks it, often loses both that and himself.

Men meet, Mountains never.

To err is human, to repent divine; to persist devilish.

The Way to see by Faith is to shut the Eye of Reason.

Changing Countries or Beds, cures neither a bad Manager, nor a Fever.

As Pride increases, Fortune declines.

Neither trust, nor contend, nor lay wagers, nor lend; and you'll have peace to your Life's end.

Happy that Nation – fortunate that age, whose history is not diverting.

Who says Jack is not generous? – he is always fond of giving, and cares not for receiving,– what? – why, advice.

When you speak to a man, look on his eyes; when he speaks to thee, look on his mouth.

There are no fools so troublesome as those that have wit.

Quarrels never could last long, if on one side only lay the wrong.

Beware, beware; he'll cheat without scruple, who can without fear.

Avoid dishonest gain: no price can recompence the pangs of vice.

Different Sects, like different clocks, may be all near the matter, 'tho they don't quite agree.

You may be too cunning for One, but not for All.

Many would live by their Wits, but break for want of stock.

Tho' Modesty is a Virtue, Bashfulness is a Vice.

Hide not your Talents, they for Use were made: What's a Sun-Dial in the Shade?

Tim was so learned, that he could name a Horse in nine Languages. So ignorant, that he bought a Cow to ride on.

Learn of the skillful: He that teaches himself, hath a fool for his master.

Anger and folly walk cheek by jowl; repentance treads on both their heels.

Well done, is twice done.

Marry above thy match, and thou'lt get a master.

Seven wealthy towns contend for Homer dead, Thro' which the living Homer begg'd his bread.

Promises may get thee friends, but non-performance will turn them into enemies.

If you'd lose a troublesome Visitor, lend him money.

Industry, Perseverance, & Frugality, make Fortune yield.

A man of knowledge, like a rich soil, feeds, If not a world of corn, a world of weeds.

Sloth (like Rust) consumes faster than Labor wears: the used Key is always bright.

Sin is not hurtful because it is forbidden, but it is forbidden because it is hurtful.

He's a Fool that cannot conceal his Wisdom.

The same man cannot be both Friend and Flatterer.

Those who are fear'd, are hated.

When man and woman die, as poets sung, his heart's the last part moves, her last, the tongue.

Do not do that which you would not have known.

He that riseth late, must trot all day, and shall scarce overtake his business at night.

There's more old drunkards, than old doctors.

He that scatters thorns, let him not go barefoot.

Reading makes a full man – Meditation a profound man – Discourse a clear man.

Many a Man thinks he is buying Pleasure, when he is really selling himself a Slave to it.

Take heed of the Vinegar of sweet Wine, and the Anger of Good-nature.

Be temperate in wine, in eating, girls, and cloth, or the Gout will seize you and plague you both.

Don't think to hunt two Hares with one Dog.

Beauty and folly are old companions.

He that cannot obey, cannot command.

An egg today is better than a hen to-morrow.

Tart Words make no Friends: a spoonful of honey will catch more flies than a Gallon of Vinegar.

The poor have little – beggars none;
The rich too much – enough not one.

To all apparent beauties blind, each
blemish strikes an envious mind.

Thou hadst better eat salt with the
philosophers of Greece, than sugar with
the courtiers of Italy.

Proclaim not all thou knowest, all thou
owest, all thou hast, nor all thou can'st.

Caesar did not merit the triumphal car
more than he that conquers himself.

Poverty wants some things, luxury
many things, avarice all things.

A Man without ceremony has need of great merit in its place.

If you'd be Wealthy, think of Saving, more than of Getting: The Indies have not made Spain rich, because her Out-goes equal her Incomes.

Old Boys have their Playthings as well as young Ones; the Difference is only in the Price.

He is not well bred, that cannot bear Ill-Breeding in others.

Eat to live; live not to eat.

After three days men grow weary of a wench, a guest, and weather rainy.

The proof of gold is fire; the proof of woman, gold; the proof of man, a woman.

At the working man's house hunger looks in, but dares not enter.

Do good to thy Friend to keep him, to thy Enemy to gain him.

You will be careful, if you are wise, how you touch men's Religion, or Credit, or Eyes.

Declaiming against Pride, is not always a Sign of Humility.

Keep Conscience clear, Then never fear.

Doing an Injury puts you below your Enemy; Revenging one makes you but even with him; Forgiving it sets you above him.

Cut the Wings of your Hens and Hopes, lest they lead you a weary Dance after them.

The Horse thinks one thing, and he that saddles him another.

Friendship cannot live with Ceremony, nor without Civility.

Would you live with ease, do what you ought, and not what you please.

Better slip with Foot than Tongue.

He that is rich need not live sparingly, and he that can live sparingly need not be rich.

The first Degree of Folly, is to conceit one's self wise; the second to profess it; the third to despise Counsel.

What is Serving God? 'Tis doing Good to Man.

A Slip of the Foot you may soon recover, but a slip of the Tongue you may never get over.

It is wise not to seek a Secret and Honest not to reveal it.

Grief often treads upon the heels of pleasure, Marry'd in haste, we oft repent at leisure; Some by experience find these words misplaced, Marry'd at leisure, they repent in haste.

A Brother may not be a Friend, but a Friend will always be a Brother.

You may talk too much on the best of subjects.

Beware of little Expenses: a small Leak will sink a great Ship.

He that lieth down with dogs, shall rise up with fleas.

He is ill clothed that is bare of virtue.

He's the best physician that knows the worthlessness of the most medicines.

There is no little enemy.

A Father's a treasure; a Brother's a comfort; a Friend is both.

What maintains one Vice would bring up two children.

A quiet Conscience sleeps in Thunder, but Rest and Guilt live far asunder.

Let thy discontents be thy secrets; – if the world knows them 'twill despise thee and increase them.

The Good-will of the Govern'd will be starved, if not fed by the good deeds of the Governors.

If you would reap Praise you must sow the Seeds: gentle Words and useful Deeds.

Many have quarrel'd about Religion, that never practiced it.

It is not Leisure that is not used.

If what most men admire they would despise, 'Twould look as if mankind were growing wise.

Kings have long Arms, but misfortune longer; let none think themselves out of her Reach.

'Tis better to leave an enemy at one's death, than beg of a friend in one's life.

He that pursues two hares at once, does not catch one and lets t'other go.

Friendship increases by visiting Friends, but by visiting seldom.

Bad Gains are true Losses.

Neglect mending a small Fault, and 'twill soon be a great One.

Beware of him that is slow to anger: He is angry for something, and will not be pleased for nothing.

A Change of Fortune hurts a wise Man no more than a Change of the Moon.

Dost thou love Life? Then do not squander Time; for that's the Stuff Life is made of.

When Knaves betray each other, one can scarce be blamed or the other pitied.

Ill thrives that hapless family that shows a cock that's silent, and a hen that crows: I know not which lives more unnatural lives, obeying husbands, or commanding wives.

If thou would'st live long, live well; for folly and wickedness shorten life.

He that pays for work before it's done, has but a pennyworth for two pence.

Thou can'st not joke an enemy into a friend, but thou may'st a friend into an enemy.

He that resolves to mend hereafter, resolves not to mend now.

When the well's dry, we know the worth of water.

An ill Wound, but not an ill Name, may be healed.

Most People return small Favors, acknowledge middling ones, and repay great ones with Ingratitude.

Youth is pert and positive, Age modest and doubting: So Ears of Corn when young and light, stand bold upright, but hang their Heads when weighty, full, and ripe.

Don't judge of Men's Wealth or Piety, by their Sunday Appearances.

The Wise and Brave dares own that he was wrong.

The busy man has few idle Visitors; to the boiling Pot the Flies come not.

Paintings and Fightings are best seen at a distance.

I never saw an oft-transplanted tree, Nor yet an oft-removed family, That throve so well as those that settled be.

Don't go to the doctor with every distemper, nor to the lawyer with every quarrel, nor to the pot for every thirst.

I saw few die of hunger; of eating – 100,000.

What is more valuable than Gold? Diamonds. Than Diamonds? Virtue.

The good or ill hap of a good or ill life, is the good or ill choice of a good or ill wife.

He that Whines for Glass without G, take away L and that's he.

You may be more happy than princes, if you will be more virtuous.

Keep your eyes wide open before marriage, half shut afterwards.

Don't throw Stones at your Neighbors if your own Windows are Glass.

Lovers, travellers, and poets, will give money to be heard.

Creditors have better memories than debtors.

There is no Man so bad but he secretly respects the Good.

Little Rogues easily become great Ones.

When the Wine enters, out goes the Truth.

Praise little, dispraise less.

Don't think so much of your own Cunning, as to forget other Men's: a Cunning Man is overmatched by a cunning Man and a Half.

To be intimate with a foolish Friend, is like going to Bed with a Razor.

'Tis a strange Forest that has no rotten Wood in't And a strange Kindred that all are good in't.

Friends are the true Scepters of Princes.

Pray don't burn my House to roast your Eggs.

Many a Man would have been worse, if his Estate had been better.

Love and Tooth-ache have many Cures, but none infallible, except Possession and Dispossession.

I have never seen the Philosopher's stone that turns lead into gold, but I have known the pursuit of it turn a man's gold into lead.

If you do what you should not, you must hear what you would not.

Now I have a sheep and a cow, every body bids me good-morrow.

A full Belly makes a dull Brain.

The Honey is sweet, but the Bee has a Sting.

A flatterer never seems absurd: The flatter'd always takes his word.

Lend money to an enemy, and thou'lt gain him; to a friend, and thou'lt lose him.

Suspicion may be no fault, but showing it may be a great one.

A good Example is the best Sermon.

Wise Men learn by other's harms; Fools by their own.

He that has a Trade has an Office of Profit and Honor.

A wise Man will desire no more than what he may get justly, use soberly, distribute cheerfully and leave contentedly.

Plough deep while Sluggards sleep; and you shall have Corn to sell and to keep.

He that's content hath enough. He that complains hath too much.

Laziness travels so slowly that Poverty soon overtakes him.

Life with Fools consists in Drinking; with the wise Man, living's Thinking.

The second Vice is Lying; the first is running in Debt.

Act uprightly and despise Calumny; Dirt may stick to a Mud Wall, but not to polish'd Marble.

Singularity in the right, hath ruined many: happy those who are convinced of the general Opinion.

Tho' the Mastiff be gentle, yet bite him not by the Lip.

Most fools think they are only ignorant.

It is Ill-manners to silence a Fool, and Cruelty to let him go on.

All would live long, but none would be old.

Nothing dries sooner than a Tear.

He that would catch Fish, must venture his Bait.

If it were not for the Belly, the Back might wear Gold.

Dally not with other Folks' Women or Money.

Tell me my Faults, and mend your own.

To be proud of Knowledge, is to be blind with Light.

Get what you can, and what you get hold; 'tis the Stone that will turn all your Lead into Gold.

An honest Man will receive neither Money nor Praise that is not his due.

He that would rise at Court, must begin by creeping.

Where there is Hunger, Law is not regarded; and where Law is not regarded, there will be Hunger.

Idleness is the Dead Sea, that swallows all Virtues: Be active in Business, that Temptation may miss her Aim; the Bird that sits, is easily shot.

Drink does not drown Care, but waters it, and makes it grow faster.

Having been poor is no shame, but being ashamed of it, is.

The wise Man draws more Advantage from his Enemies, than the Fool from his Friends.

Work as if you were to live 100 years, Pray as if you were to die Tomorrow.

Men take more pains to mask than mend.

Avarice and happiness never saw each other; how then should they become acquainted?

Keep thy shop, and thy shop will keep thee.

When Knaves fall out, honest men get their goods: When Priests dispute, we come at the Truth.

How many observe Christ's Birthday; How few his Precepts! O, 'tis easier to keep Holidays than Commandments.

One good Husband is worth two good Wives; for the scarcer things are, the more they're valued.

Dine with little, sup with less: Do better still: sleep supperless.

Many Foxes grow grey, but few grow good.

What signifies knowing the Names, if you know not the Natures of Things?

Be not niggardly of what costs thee nothing, as courtesy, counsel, and countenance.

Love and Lordship hate companions.

The family of Fools is ancient.

There are three faithful friends – an old wife, an old dog, and ready money.

We keep the vices of others in sight; our own we carry on our backs.

Silence is not always a Sign of Wisdom, but Babbling is ever a Folly.

Mine is better than Ours.

Be always ashamed to catch thyself idle.

Pay what you owe, and what you're worth you'll know.

A Pair of good Ears will drink dry a hundred Tongues.

Many complain of their Memory, few of their Judgment.

Fear God, and your Enemies will fear you.

Pride dines upon Vanity, sups on Contempt.

Let no pleasure tempt thee, no profit allure thee, no ambition corrupt thee, no example sway thee, no persuasion move thee, to do any thing which thou knowest to be evil; so shalt thou always live jollily; for a good conscience is a continual Christmas.

He that won't be counsell'd, can't be help'd.

Nothing humbler than Ambition, when it is about to climb.

A house without woman and firelight, is like a body without soul or sprite.

Craft must be at charge for clothes, but Truth can go naked.

He that buys by the penny, maintains not only himself, but other people.

The Morning Daylight appears plainer when you put out your Candle.

If any man flatters me, I'll flatter him again, though he were my best friend.

Fools need Advice most, but only wise Men are the better for it.

Sudden Power is apt to be insolent, Sudden Liberty saucy; that behaves best which has grown gradually.

Half-Wits talk much but say little.

After crosses and losses, men grow humbler and wiser.

A good lawyer, a bad neighbor.

Eat few Suppers, and you'll need few Medicines.

If Passion drives, let Reason hold the Reins.

Here comes Glib-Tongue who can out-flatter a Dedication and lie like 10 Epitaphs.

There are lazy minds as well as lazy bodies.

Clean your Finger, before you point at my Spots.

Great Merit is coy, as well as great Pride.

Praise to the undeserving, is severe Satire.

He's gone, and forgot nothing but to say farewell to his creditors.

Great talkers, little doers.

O Lazy bones! Dost thou think God would have given thee arms and legs, if he had not design'd thou should'st use them?

Epitaph on a Scolding Wife by her Husband: Here my poor Bridget's Corpse doth lie, she is at rest,—and so am I.

Where carcasses are, eagles will gather; where good Laws are, much people flock thither.

All blood is alike ancient.

If your head is wax, don't walk in the Sun.

Up, sluggard, and waste not life; in the grave will be sleeping enough.

You can bear your own Faults, and why not a Fault in your Wife.

They who have nothing to trouble them, will be troubled at nothing.

Neglect kills Injuries, Revenge increases them.

There is much money given to be laughed at, though the purchasers don't know it; witness A's fine horse, and B's fine house.

Strange! that a Man who has wit enough to write a Satire, should have folly enough to publish it.

He that takes a wife takes Care.

Teach your child to hold his tongue, he'll learn fast enough to speak.

Lost time is never found again.

Who is strong? He that can conquer his bad Habits.

Against Diseases here, the strongest
    Fence,
Is the defensive Virtue, Abstinence.
If thou dost ill, the joy fades, not the
    pains;
If well, the pain doth fade, the joy
    remains.

Seek Virtue, and of that possessed, to Providence resign the rest.

What is a Butterfly?—at best he's but a caterpillar dressed—The gaudy Fop's his picture just.

Now that you have read, most *Honest Reader*, this rich & saucy Sampling of the various Editions of Ben Franklin's famed *Almanacks*, there remains for you to meet its *Designer*, one *Harald Peter*; to know that it has been set, for Clarity & Antiqueness of Appearance & for your Reading Pleasure, in 14 point *Monotype Walbaum*; that it has been printed on a most pleasant paper known by its Trade Name, *viz., Hallmark Eggshell Book*; & that it was printed, like the Original Almanacks, in the United States of *America*.